THREE BRIDGES
TO
BRIGHTON

Vic Mitchell and Keith Smith

Cover design – Deborah Goodridge

First published October 1986

ISBN 0 906520 35 5

© Middleton Press, 1986

Typeset by CitySet - Bosham 573270

Published by Middleton Press
          Easebourne Lane
          Midhurst, West Sussex
          GU29 9AZ
          ☎ *073 081 3169*

Printed & bound by Biddles Ltd,
          Guildford and Kings Lynn

CONTENTS

ACKNOWLEDGEMENTS

We are grateful for the help received from many of those mentioned in the photograph credits and also L. Oppitz, R. Randell and R. Resch. We thank Mrs. E. Wallis for use of her late husband's photographs. As in our other albums covering former LBSCR lines, we benefit from the researches of members of the Brighton Circle. Our gratitude is also expressed to Mrs. E. Fisk, N. Stanyon and our wives for help in production. Tickets come from the collections of N. Langridge and G. Croughton.

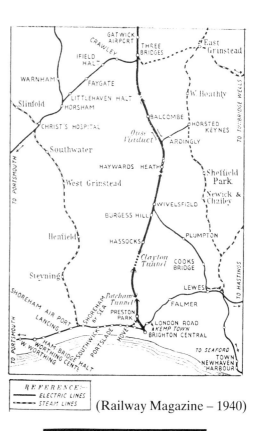

(Railway Magazine – 1940)

GEOGRAPHICAL SETTING

Three Bridges is at the northern boundary of the highland formed by the sandstone of the Hastings beds, which stretch west to Horsham. This dome of the Central Weald is penetrated by Balcombe Tunnel, south of which the line drops steadily until reaching the Wealden Clay, around Wivelsfield. After traversing this relatively level area, the route starts its climb to Clayton Tunnel, which pierces the chalk mass of the South Downs. A steady descent, entirely on chalk land takes the line to its terminus, which is about 100ft. above sea level.

There are few rivers of note on the route, although the depth of the valley of the small River Ouse north of Haywards Heath necessitated the construction of a substantial viaduct.

All maps in this album are to the scale of 25″ to one mile, unless otherwise stated.

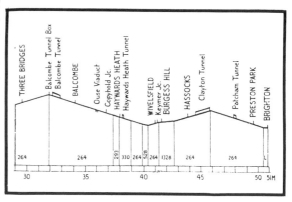

HISTORICAL BACKGROUND

An extension of the London & Croydon Railway southwards to Haywards Heath was brought into use by the London & Brighton Railway Co. on 12th July 1841. The route to Brighton was completed on 21st September of that year, linking it with the line along the coast to Shoreham. This had been opened the previous year to facilitate transport of construction materials from the nearby harbour.

In 1846, the company's name was changed to the London, Brighton & South Coast Railway Co. and branches were added southwards as follows:

From	To	Opened
Three Bridges	*Horsham*	*14-2-1848*
Three Bridges	*E. Grinstead*	*9-7-1855*
Copyhold Junc.	*Horsted Keynes*	*3-9-1883*
Keymer Junc.	*Lewes*	*1-10-1847*
Brighton	*Lewes*	*8-6-1846*

Passenger services were withdrawn from the East Grinstead branch on 1st January 1967 and from the Horsted Keynes line on 28th October 1963.

The most notable event in the history of the main line was the introduction of electric services south of Three Bridges on 1st January 1933.

PASSENGER SERVICES

Initially four trains each way were provided between London Bridge and Haywards Heath on weekdays, with two on Sundays, and a connecting road coach was available to and from Brighton. The through service between London and Brighton commenced with six return journeys, the 8.30 a.m. up being an express for "business people" – an important traffic ever since. Three trains were operated each way on Sundays.

In the early years several trains were first class only, a type of traffic the company wished to foster, but eventually circumstances demanded the provision of mass transit at the other end of the market.

Through coaches to Shoreham were introduced in 1844, but for first class passengers only. Parliament required all railways to operate one train a day in which "the lower orders" could travel at one penny (1d) per mile. In 1845 the "Parly" was inconveniently timed to leave London at 6.30 a.m.

By 1856, the service had increased to 12 weekday and three Sunday trains each way. From 1858, trains ran to London Bridge or Battersea, the latter services being extended to Victoria in 1860. The timetable was little different in 1865, with most trains being divided at Croydon for the two London termini. At this time, additional trains were introduced between London and Brighton, running via Horsham and Shoreham, and the main line services began operating at regular intervals. From 1867, two of the London Bridge trains were extended to Cannon Street.

1875 was notable for the introduction of a Pullman Car on selected trains and 1876 saw the start of a third class only service, once a day, from Liverpool Street via the East London line, which was operated by the LBSCR.

The opening of the Cliftonville spur in 1879 reduced the congestion at Brighton station caused by the reversal of trains to and from Hove. The first all-Pullman trains on the LBSCR commenced on 1st December 1881 and were largely electrically lit. By the early 1890s, traffic had increased to the point that complete trains were run to the London termini and splitting at Croydon was largely eliminated. At this time, slip coaches were widely used, notably at Haywards Heath, where down trains shed coaches for Eastbourne.

At the turn of the century the main line carried two first class only, four first and second class and 24 trains carrying all three classes. These were also through trains via Horsham, Ardingly and Lewes and some of the direct services were divided at Preston Park for Hove and stations west. Sundays saw seven direct all-classes trains and the "Brighton Limited" Pullman from Victoria completed the journey in exactly one hour.

The "Sunny South Special" was introduced in 1904, being operated in conjunction with LNWR to and from Manchester and Liverpool via Kensington Addison Road (now Olympia). An experimental service to Paddington was tried in 1906–07, also running via Addison Road. New coaches for the all Pullman trains were supplied in the following year, when the train was renamed the "Southern Belle", a name which was retained until electrification when the

"Brighton Belle" was introduced.

1912 saw the withdrawal of second class accommodation and the provision of a departure from Victoria at five minutes past midnight, the railway thus reflecting the social changes of the time.

During the first summer of the Southern Railway (1923) there were 31 down and 28 up trains on weekdays, with extras on Saturdays and, on Sundays, there were 14 down and 16 up.

Electrification in 1933 brought a remarkable increase in frequency. The basic service from Victoria each hour comprised two expresses (one of which ran direct to West Worthing); one semi-fast and one stopping train. There was also a semi-fast and a stopping train from London Bridge. Electrification of the Eastbourne and Hastings services in 1935 added an express calling at Haywards Heath and a stopping service between Horsted Keynes and Seaford.

With the advent of WWII, the through trains to Worthing and Eastbourne were reduced, as were North of England trains and buffet services. The latter were withdrawn totally in May 1942, and other services reduced.

Steam operated passenger trains from the Midlands and North reached their zenith in the 1950s, being particularly numerous on summer Saturdays. Steam was abolished in October 1965 at the time when the second generation of electric stock was being introduced. Pullman services were withdrawn in 1972, by which year journey times had been slightly reduced.

In May 1978, a full revision of the services took place, but the frequency of service to Brighton remained the same with one fast, one semi-fast and two stopping trains per hour. Both of the latter then served Victoria – the London Bridge service has been restored subsequently. All trains then called at East Croydon and, in the following year, direct Manchester services were resumed.

1. LBSCR class B4 no. 46 stands at Paddington with the through service from Brighton in 1907. Note the perambulators of the period and the transparency of the GWR employee, due to his departure during the long photographic exposure. The route of the train included the spur between the Metropolitan Railway at Latimer Road and the West London Line at Uxbridge Road.
(E.R. Lacey collection)

GREAT WESTERN RAILWAY.

Circular No. 1658.

OFFICE OF SUPERINTENDENT OF THE LINE,
PADDINGTON STATION,

June, 1906.

THROUGH TRAIN
BETWEEN
BRIGHTON and PADDINGTON.

Commencing on Monday, July 2nd, a THROUGH TRAIN will be run between BRIGHTON and PADDINGTON, at the undermentioned times, giving connections to and from Hove, Worthing, Eastbourne, Hastings, &c. :—

				a.m.						p.m.
BRIGHTON	...	dep.	11 30	PADDINGTON	...	dep.	3 40
Croydon	...	,,	12 31	Latimer Road	...	pass	3 46½
Clapham Junction	...	,,	12 45	Kensington (Addison Road)	...	arr.	3 50
Kensington (Addison Road) **T**	...	arr.	12 53	,, ,, ,,	...	dep.	3 54
,, ,, ,, ...	...	dep.	12 56	Clapham Junction	...	,,	4 7
Latimer Road...	...	pass	1 3	Croydon	...	,,	4 23
PADDINGTON	...	arr.	1 10	BRIGHTON	...	arr.	5 17

T Collect Tickets.

The Train will consist of London Brighton & South Coast Company's Engine and Stock, formed as follows :—

	SEATING CAPACITY.			
	1st Class.	2nd Class.	3rd Class.	TOTAL.
Van Third	—	—	50	
Second	—	80	—	
Compo. 1st and 2nd ...	32	40	—	
Tri-Compo. ... ,...	10	20	40	
Van Third	—	—	35	
	42	140	125	= 307

Passengers will be booked through between Great Western and London, Brighton & South Coast Company's Stations, and Station Masters must instruct the Booking Clerks, Luggage Labellers, Stowers and Station Staff to be careful to advise passengers of the times of the service, and label and stow the luggage for transfer at Paddington.

Luggage must be labelled through via Paddington.

For further information as to the Train Service, see page 2 of the Penny Time Book for July.

THROUGH BOOKINGS are in operation between Paddington and other principal Great Western Stations and the principal stations on the London Brighton & South Coast Railway. Other through fares can be arranged as required and any stations having enquiry for through fares must immediately make application to me for the same.

PARCELS, Etc. Parcels, Dogs, Bicycles and other similar traffic to or from the L. B. & S. C. Railway may be conveyed by these Trains. The service will also form a ready means of transit for all traffic to land from that Company's Line.

For the present, Horse and Carriage Traffic will not be conveyed to or from Paddington by this Service.

The Staff generally are desired to make themselves acquainted with these arrangements, and to make them known to the travelling public.

Acknowledge receipt to Head of Department.

J. MORRIS,
Superintendent of the Line.

Printed at the Company's Office, 150, Westbourne Terrace, Paddington, W.

LONDON AND BRIGHTON RAILWAY.

DOWN TRAINS. — LONDON TO BRIGHTON.

Distance.	Station	Daily, except Sundays: 9¾ A.M. Mixed Train.	10¾ A.M. First Class Train.	1¾ P.M. Mixed Train.	2¾ P.M. Mixed Train.	3¾ P.M. First Class Train.	4¾ P.M. Express Train.	7 P.M. Mixed Train to Croydon.	Sunday Trains: 8 A.M. Mixed Train.	10¾ A.M. Mixed Train.	7 P.M. Mixed Train.	10 P.M. Mixed Train to Croydon.
Miles.		H. M.	H. M.	H. M.	H. M.	H. M.	H. M.	H. M.	H. M.	A. M.	H. M.	H. M.
	*LONDON	9.45	10.45	1.45	2.45	3.45	4.45	7. 0	8. 0	10.45	7. 0	10. 0
3	*New Cross	9.53	....	1.53	2 53	....	....	....	8. 8	10.53	7. 8	....
10¼	*CROYDON	10.15	11. 8	2.15	3.15	4. 8	....	7.30	8.30	11.15	7 30	10.30
13¼	Godstone Road	10.26	....	2.26	3.26	....	....	....	8.41	11.26	7.41	....
14½	Stoat's Nest	10.31	....	2.31	3.31	....	....	...	8.46	11.31	7.46	...
19½	Merstham	10.45	....	2.45	3.45	....	...	....	9. 0	11.45	8. 0	....
21¼	*RED HILL	10.51	11.35	2.51	3.51	4.35	....	.. .	9. 6	11.51	8. 6	....
25½	*Horley	11. 3	....	3. 3	4. 3	....	....	....	9.18	12. 3	8.18	....
29¼	*THREE BRIDGES	11.15	11.56	3.15	4.15	4.56	....	...	9.30	12.15	8.30	....
33¼	Balcombe	11.27	....	3.27	4.27	....	....	....	9.42	12.27	8.42	....
37¾	*HAYWARD'S HEATH	11.38	12.15	3.38	4.38	5.15	....	....	9.53	12.38	8.53	....
43½	Hassock's Gate	11.54	....	3.54	4.54	....	....	....	10. 9	12.54	9. 9	....
50½	*BRIGHTON	12.15	12.45	4.15	5.15	5.45	6.30	....	10.30	1.15	9.30	....

Station	Fares — Passengers: First Class.	Second Class.	Children in Second Class.	Carriages: Four Wheels.	Two Wheels.	Horses: One Horse.	Two Horses. (If belonging to One Party.)	Three Horses. (If belonging to One Party.)
	s. d.	s. d.	s. d.	s. d.	s. d.	s. d.	s. d.	s. d.
*LONDON	....	....	....	....	....	....	....	....
*New Cross	....	....	....	....	....	....	....	....
*CROYDON	2 0	1 6	1 6	12 6	10 0	10 0	15 0	20 0
Godstone Road	3 6	2 4	1 8	....	....	....	....	....
Stoat's Nest	4 0	2 8	2 0	....	....	....	....	....
Merstham	5 0	3 8	2 6	....	....	....	....	....
*RED HILL	5 6	4 0	2 8	15 0	12 0	12 0	18 0	24 0
*Horley	7 0	5 0	3 4	17 0	14 0	14 0	21 0	28 0
*THREE BRIDGES	8 0	5 6	3 8	20 0	16 0	16 0	24 0	32 0
Balcombe	9 0	6 4	4 4	....	....	....	....	....
*HAYWARD'S HEATH	10 6	7 0	4 8	25 0	20 0	20 0	30 0	40 0
Hassock's Gate	12 6	8 0	5 6	....	....	....	....	....
*BRIGHTON	14 6	9 6	6 6	32 0	25 0	25 0	38 0	50 0

N.B.—No Passengers will be conveyed from London to New Cross, or from New Cross to London.

UP TRAINS. — BRIGHTON TO LONDON.

Distance.	Station	Daily, except Sundays: 6¾ A.M. Mixed Train.	8½ A.M. Express Train.	10¾ A.M. First Class Train.	11¾ A.M. Mixed Train.	Mixed Train from Croydon.	2¼ P.M. First Class Train.	4 P.M. Mixed Train.	Sunday Trains: Mixed Train from Croydon.	7¾ A.M. Mixed Train.	4 P.M. Mixed Train.	7 P.M. Mixed Train.
Miles.		H. M.	H. M.	H. M.	H. M.	H. M.	H. M.	H. M.	H. M.	H. M.	H. M.	H. M.
	*BRIGHTON	6.45	8.30	10.45	11.45	......	2.15	4. 0	......	7.45	4. 0	7. 0
7	Hassock's Gate	7. 3	....	....	12. 3	......	....	4.18	......	8. 3	4.18	7.18
12¾	*HAYWARD'S HEATH	7.21	..:.	11. 9	12.21	......	2.39	4.36	......	8.21	4.36	7.36
17	Balcombe	7.35	....	....	12.35	......	....	4.50	......	8.35	4.50	7.50
21¼	*THREE BRIDGES	7.46	....	11.31	12.46	......	3. 1	5. 1	......	8.46	5. 1	8. 1
25	*Horley	7.56	....	....	12.56	......	....	5.11	......	8.56	5.11	8.11
29¼	*RED HILL	8.10	....	1[illegible]53	1.10	......	3.23	5.25	......	9.10	5.25	8.25
31	Merstham	8.17	....	....	1.17	......	....	5.32	......	9.17	5.32	8.32
36	Stoat's Nest	8.30	....	....	1.30	......	....	5.45	......	9.30	5.45	8.45
37¼	Godstone Road	8.34	....	....	1.34	......	....	5.49	......	9.34	5.49	8.49
40¼	*CROYDON	8.42	....	12.18	1.42	2.45	3.48	5.57	7. 0	9.42	5.57	8.57
47½	*New Cross	9. 5	....	....	2. 5	3. 5	....	6 20	7.20	10. 5	6.20	9.20
50½	*LONDON	9.15	10.15	12.45	2.15	3.15	4.15	6.30	7.30	10.15	6.30	9.30

Station	Fares — Passengers: First Class.	Second Class.	Children in Second Class.	Carriages: Four Wheels.	Two Wheels.	Horses: One Horse.	Two Horses. (If belonging to one Party.)	Three Horses. (If belonging to one Party.)
	s. d.	s. d.	s. d.	s. d.	s. d.	s. d.	s. d	s. d.
*BRIGHTON	....	....	......	....	....	....	....	....
Hassock's Gate	2 0	1 6	1 0	....	....	....	....	....
*HAYWARD'S HEATH	3 6	2 6	1 8	12 6	10 0	10 0	15 0	20 0
Balcombe	4 8	3 4	2 4	....	....	....	....	....
*THREE BRIDGES	6 0	4 0	2 8	15 0	12 0	12 0	18 0	24 0
*Horley	7 0	4 8	3 4	17 0	14 0	14 0	21 0	28 0
*RED HILL	8 6	5 6	3 8	20 0	16 0	16 0	24 0	32 0
Merstham	9 0	6 0	4 0	....	....	....	....	....
Stoat's Nest	10 6	7 0	4 6	....	....	....	....	....
Godstone Road	10 8	7 4	4 8	....	....	....	....	....
*CROYDON	11 8	8 0	5 0	26 0	21 0	21 0	32 0	42 0
*New Cross	13 8	9 0	6 0	....	....	....	....	....
*LONDON	14 6	9 6	6 6	32 0	25 0	25 0	38 0	50 0

THE EXPRESS AND FIRST CLASS TRAINS will consist of *First Class Carriages only*, except that two compartments of the leading carriage will be reserved for Servants in attendance on their Employers, at Second Class Fares.

THE EXPRESS TRAIN will stop no where on the line to take up or set down Passengers, and no Private Carriages or Horses will be conveyed by it.
THE FIRST CLASS TRAINS will stop at *First Class Stations only* (designated in the above Table by Capital Letters) but they will take Private Carriages and Horses (belonging to Passengers in the Train) only from London to Brighton, or Brighton to London.
THE MIXED TRAINS will consist of both First and Second Class Carriages; they will all take up and set down Passengers at *every Station on the Line*; and Carriages and Horses will be conveyed by them to and from all the Carriage Stations (marked thus *.)
A Carriage with First Class Coupées will be provided for the accommodation of Families, or Parties engaging them.

September 1841.

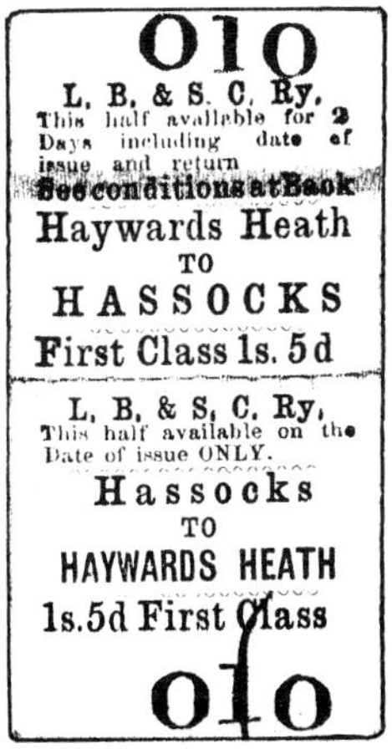

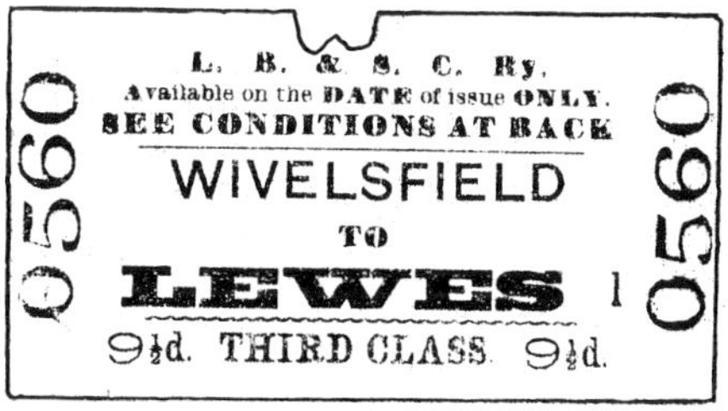

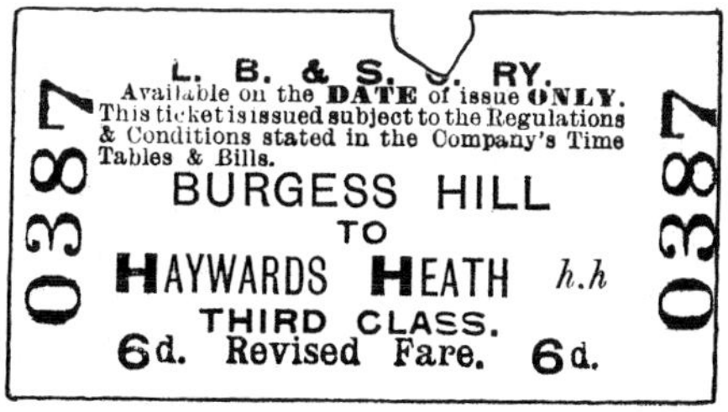

THREE BRIDGES

The 1911 edition shows two turntables (45ft. and 60ft.) and two engine sheds. The earlier shed, seen in photograph no.4, was situated west of the platforms, close to the pump house.

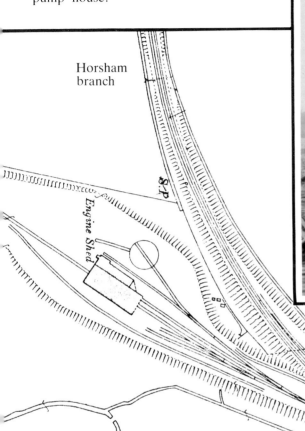

Horsham branch

Engine Shed

GHTON & SOUTH COAST RAILWAY

F.P.

2. The station was called "Crawley" until the Horsham branch was opened in 1848. Class B2 no. 213 waits to depart south, whilst another train waits in the up loop. The roof over the loop was lost when the lines were quadrupled around 1908.
(W.G. Tilling/R.C. Riley collection)

3. Numerous improvements were undertaken over the years. The original single
storey building was doubled in height in 1867
and refreshment rooms were eventually provided on all three platforms. (Lens of Sutton)

L. B. & S. C. RY.
Available on the DATE of issue ONLY
This ticket is issued subject to the Regulation
& Conditions stated in the Company's Time
Tables & Bills.
THREE BRIDGES
TO
LINGFIELD L.
THIRD CLASS.
1/6 Revised Fare. 1/6
2824

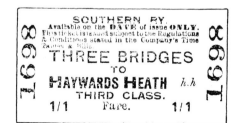

SOUTHERN RY.
Available on the DATE of issue ONLY.
This ticket is issued subject to the Regulations
& Conditions stated in the Company's Time
Tables & Bills.
THREE BRIDGES
TO
HAYWARDS HEATH h.h
THIRD CLASS.
1/1 Fare. 1/1
1698

4. An 1898 photograph shows the last Craven designed engine in service, albeit immobilised beside the locomotive shed as a source of steam for the water pump. It had been built at Brighton in 1866 and was broken up in 1901. (E.R. Lacey collection)

5. The quadrupling work took place between 1907 and 1911. When complete, new station offices and the station master's house were built on the west side of the line. They are not shown on the 1911 Ordnance Survey but remain in use today. (Lens of Sutton)

6. A southward view shows the East Grinstead line diverging on the left and some of the ten down sidings behind Central Box. The Horsham line is shown diverging on the right. (Lens of Sutton)

7. The northward scene from Central Box in 1928 includes cattle pens on the left, also the new island platform for the up loop and up local lines. On the right are the sidings of the goods yard, the most easterly one passing through a gate to the corn mills, the structure of which still stands today. (Late E. Wallis)

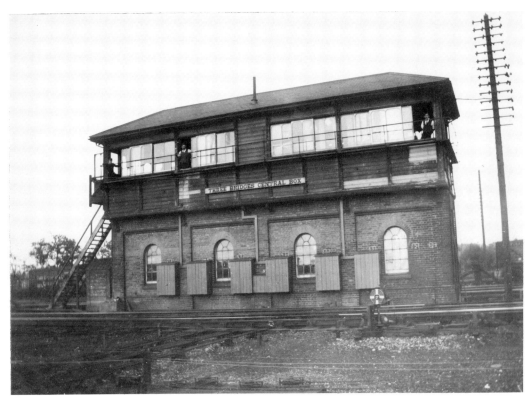

8. A closer look at Central Box in 1928 shows it to be of timber construction on a brick machine room. A typical LBSCR ground signal is in the foreground. (Late E. Wallis)

9. Electric services south to Three Bridges started on 17th July 1932 and were extended to Brighton and West Worthing on 1st January 1933. This is the last day of main line steam with "King Arthur" 4–6–0 no. E798 *Sir Hectimere* on a Victoria to Brighton semi-fast and class I1 4–4–2T no. B2 in the siding. (Lens of Sutton)

10. Steam persisted on freight, parcels and inter-regional trains. This example is class N no. 31813 with the 5.00am stone train from Salisbury on 3rd May 1958. (D. Cullum)

11. The third locomotive shed at Three Bridges had three roads and came into use in about 1909. Class C2X no. 32535, with its extra dome, is seen being refuelled by the coaling crane on 5th March 1961. (R.C. Riley)

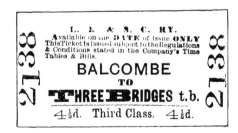

12. Another view of the south end of the shed (in April 1963) reveals the locomotive hoist and the curved roof of the machine shop. With these facilities, fairly major mechanical repairs could be undertaken. The shed closed in June 1964, after which motive power was provided from Brighton. (J. Scrace)

13. From 1955 the steam-operated services radiating from East Grinstead were time-tabled to a regular hourly interval. BR class 4 no. 80032 departs for Tunbridge Wells West at 17.08 on 8th October 1965. (J. Scrace)

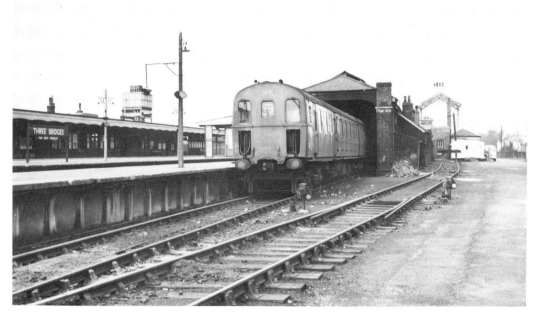

14. The service to Tunbridge Wells was withdrawn on 1st January 1967, having been operated in its final years by DEMUs of the type seen here, in the down bay. Other views of this station are to be found in our *Branch Lines to East Grinstead*. (J. Scrace)

15. This signal box stood at the down end of platforms 1 and 2 from 1955 until 1986. From 11th July 1983, the route south to Keymer Junction was signalled from an even less photogenic building on the opposite side of the main line. The appendanges housed the relay room, the S & T mess room and tool room. The separate building on the platform end was the announcer's cabin. (J. Scrace)

16. No. 47262 hauls the 07.30 Treherbert to Bognor Regis excursion past Balcombe Tunnel Box on 11th June 1978. It was diverted to Eastbourne due to a derailment at Hove. Quadruple track ends at this point and the siding on the left is provided for the Engineer's use, terminating near the sub-station seen in the next picture. (J. Scrace)

17. The 07.25 Brighton to New Cross Gate van train is seen from Parish Lane bridge, behind no. 73006 on 24th June 1978. To allow faster running, the track curvature was reduced by moving the junction north of the bridge in 1981. (J. Scrace)

18. The expense of duplicating Balcombe Tunnel has prevented quadruple track being taken further south. The up Newhaven boat train emerges from within the Wealden sandstones on 15th June 1968, behind no. E6041. (J. Scrace)

MURDER.

£200 REWARD.

WHEREAS, on Monday, June 27th, ISAAC FREDERICK GOULD was murdered on the London Brighton and South Coast Railway, between Three Bridges and Balcombe, in East Sussex.

AND WHEREAS a Verdict of WILFUL MURDER has been returned by a Coroner's Jury against

PERCY LEFROY MAPLETON,

whose Portrait and Handwriting are given hereon,—

and who is described as being 22 years of age, height 5 ft. 8 or 9 in., very thin, hair (cut short) dark, small dark whiskers; dress dark frock coat, and shoes, and supposed low black hat (worn at back of head), had scratches from fingers on throat, several wounds on head, the dressing of which involved the cutting of hair; recently lodged at 4, Cathcart Road, Wallington, was seen at 9.30 a.m., 28th ult., with his head bandaged, at the Fever Hospital, Liverpool Road, Islington. Had a gold open-faced watch (which he is likely to pledge). "Maker, Griffiths, Mile End Road, No. 16261."

One Half of the above Reward will be paid by Her Majesty's Government, and One Half by the Directors of the London Brighton and South Coast Railway, to any person (other than a person belonging to a Police Force in the United Kingdom) who shall give such information as shall lead to the discovery and apprehension of the said PERCY LEFROY MAPLETON, or others, the Murderer, or Murderers, upon his or their conviction; and the Secretary of State for the Home Department will advise the grant of Her Majesty's gracious PARDON to any accomplice, not being the person who actually committed the Murder, who shall give such evidence as shall lead to a like result.

Information to be given to the Chief Constable of East Sussex, Lewes, at any Police Station, or to

The Director of Criminal Investigations, Gt. Scotland Yard.

JULY 4th, 1881.

BALCOMBE

19. An 1892 photograph shows the drops in the platform edges that were provided to assist passengers using the foot crossing prior to the erection of a foot bridge. In 1986, the station remained the sole surviving unspoilt country station on the route, complete with its independent gentleman's toilet block, featured in this view. The first station was to the north of the present one which was built in 1848 and extended in 1869 by the addition of a new booking office and waiting room.
(Mrs. G.J. Smith collection)

Lefroy Mapleton robbed an elderly businessman of 5s.6d. and a gold watch, jettisoning his body from the train while it was passing through Balcombe Tunnel. The bloodstained murderer alighted at Preston Park, complaining that *he* had been attacked on the journey. After trial at Maidstone, he finally admitted guilt and was hanged.

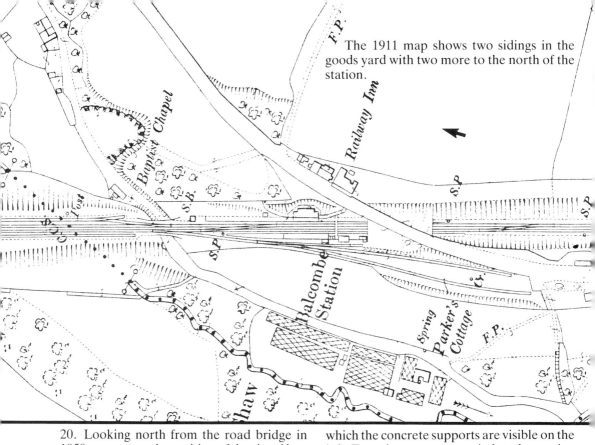

The 1911 map shows two sidings in the goods yard with two more to the north of the station.

Baptist Chapel

Railway Inn

Balcombe Station

Spring

Parker's Cottage

F.P.

20. Looking north from the road bridge in 1950, we can see the position of the signal box and the down siding beyond it. Between 1950 and 1959, one of the other sidings was electrified with overhead conductor wire for which the concrete supports are visible on the left. Experiments were carried out here using the former SR electric locomotives fitted with pantographs. (R.C. Riley)

21. This 1961 view shows the former position of the down side entrance and the covered steps leading down to the platform and foot- bridge. The latter was subsequently replaced by a concrete one, moved from the former Gatwick Racecourse station. (D. Cullum)

22. The replacement footbridge was erected on the site of the former station house and a new path provided to the road. With the loss of the sidings, both platforms were extended northwards. DEMU no. 1203 is seen on 30th May 1968, bound for St. Leonards, via Eastbourne, for servicing. (J. Scrace)

23. Balcombe Intermediate Box was on the up side, 400yds south of Balcombe Tunnel. The next box was Stone Hall seen here in 1932. It was nearly 1½ miles south of Balcombe, on the down side.
(Late E. Wallis)

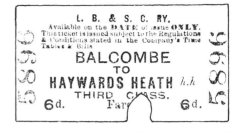

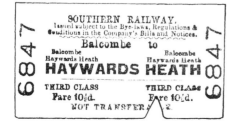

25. Each one of the 37 piers has a different height aperture in it. Most of the millions of bricks required were brought from temporary brick fields by means of small barges on the River Ouse. (J. Scrace)

26. One of the four temples that adorn each end of the structure once provided an ideal venue for an enthusiastic railway photographer. He was delighted to find a class D1 tank coming towards him, light engine. He was less pleased to find that it stopped beside him and that it carried a railway policeman who promptly arrested him. (R.C. Riley)

OUSE VALLEY VIADUCT

24. The graceful form of the viaduct cannot be enjoyed by railway passengers but they can feast their eyes on the view down the valley towards Ardingly College. The down Newhaven boat train speeds south on 22nd July 1951, behind class U1 2–6–0 no. 31909. (S.C. Nash)

COPYHOLD JUNCTION

27. In 1883, a branch was built from Haywards Heath to Horsted Keynes to connect with the Lewes to East Grinstead line, part of which is now the Bluebell Line. For many years, the double track ran parallel to the main lines as far as Haywards Heath. Class B1 no. 193 *Fremantle* runs south with a train of six-wheelers from Ardingly, the only intermediate station on the branch.
(Lens of Sutton)

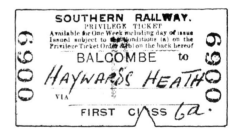

SOUTHERN RAILWAY.
PRIVILEGE TICKET
Available for One Week including day of issue
Issued subject to conditions (a) on the
Privilege Ticket Order (b) on the back hereof
0069 BALCOMBE to 0069
HAYWARDS HEATH
VIA
FIRST CLASS 6a.

1334 SOUTHERN RAILWAY. 1334
BALCOMBE
The holder is prohibited from entering
the Companies Trains. Not Transferable
Admit ONE PLATFORM 1ᴰ
Available ONE HOUR only ISSUE ONLY
This Ticket must be given up on leaving Platform.
FOR CONDITIONS SEE BACK.
1 2 3 4 5 6

29. Passenger services were withdrawn from the branch on 28th October 1963 but a single line was retained as far as Ardingly to serve a roadstone depot. Two of the three 5-coach all Pullman sets are seen passing the S & T relay room on 24th February 1968.
(E. Wilmshurst)

28. LBSCR class I1 no. 9 became B9 in SR stock – B for Brighton. A junction was provided in 1912 but it was not until electrification that the running arrangements were altered so that the two outer tracks were used by London stopping trains and the branch service. (Lens of Sutton)

30. Serious disruption of services followed a collision on 16th December 1972, when the 21.28 from Brighton, an up local train, passed red signals and the 21.45, an express from Brighton, ran into the side of it. Thanks to the excellent impact resistance of modern rolling stock, there were no serious injuries. (G. Milton)

The 1881 map shows a siding terminating in the road outside the west front of the station. The fan of three sidings on the down side served a coal wharf. The line to it was laid on the site of a railway signal factory run by Mr. Saxby. His enforced move in about 1860 caused him to seek finance from Mr. Farmer and thus began the world-famous signalling firm.

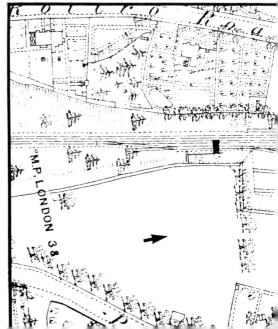

HAYWARDS HEATH

31. The coming of the railway transformed a thinly populated area into a country market town and eventually into a massive residential area. The middle phase is illustrated by this post card of the west side of the station and the Station Hotel, beyond which is the cattle market. (Lens of Sutton)

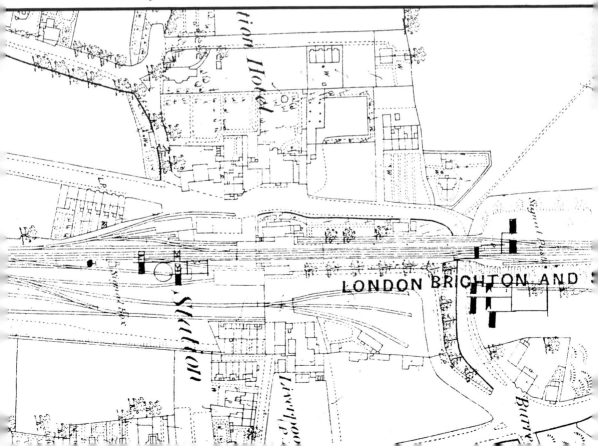

32. South Box is in the distance and the up bay is on the right of this photograph which details the gas lights and water crane. A wheel on the latter ran in a double inclined plane which thus automatically self-centred the arm to prevent it accidentally touching trains. (Lens of Sutton)

33. Larger platform canopies were added in 1863 but the goods shed in the background was demolished to make way for station expansion prior to electrification. (Lens of Sutton)

34. The rural surroundings are evident in this hill-top view, as are the two signal boxes and busy goods yard. Careful study of the map will show that the station had entrances on both sides of the line. (Lens of Sutton)

35. A 1930 photograph reveals that the down bay line was partly roofed over, as at Three Bridges. It was used by stopping trains to Brighton that departed after having connected with down London expresses. There is also a good record of the goods shed and cattle pens. (Late E. Wallis)

36. Former LBSCR class E4 no. B491 runs past North Box on 19th July 1930, with a train from the Horsted Keynes branch. The leading coach is of the Birdcage type, examples of which survive today on the nearby Bluebell Railway. (H.C. Casserley)

L. B. & S. C. RY.
Available on the **DATE** of issue **ONLY.**
This Ticket is issued subject to the Regulations & Conditions stated in the Company's Time Tables & Bills.

HAYWARDS Heath

TO

THREE BRIDGES t.b.

FIRST CLASS.

2/4 Revised Fare. **2/4**

1223   1223

SOUTHERN RAILWAY.
Available on the **DATE** of issue **ONLY**
This Ticket is issued subject to the Regulations & Conditions stated in the Company's Time Tables & Bills.

HAYWARDS HEATH

TO

WEST GRINSTEAD w.g

THIRD CLASS.

3/1 Fare. **3/1**

0012   0012

UP] L. B. & S. C. RY.
Ticket for BICYCLE at Owners Risk when accompanied by passenger.

HAYWARDS H'TH.

To any Station on the
L.B.&S.C.R. not exceeding **12** miles.

RATE 1/0

This Ticket is available for a single Journey Only, and must be given up on arrival.

0449   0449

Many other views of both this station and the next one are to be found in our *Haywards Heath to Seaford* album in this series. Other pictures of the route appear in *Steaming through East Sussex.*

---

39. The latest from the motor car showrooms grace the forecourt of the new station in 1932, whilst the new asbestos-clad goods shed just appears in the background. The then common style of telephone kiosk is now a rarity – one survives in Bembridge, Isle of Wight. (N. Langridge collection)

37. Looking south from the down platform in 1930, we can see a small shunt signal level with the windows of South Box and also look right through the tunnel. This is 249 yards long and variously known as Folly Hill or Haywards Heath Tunnel. (Late E. Wallis)

38. Prior to the 1933 electrification, extensive reconstruction took place. Here we witness placement of the new bridge spans, close to North Box, and excavation taking place for the new station offices. The wooden wagons were hauled away by steam tractor. (G. Milton collection)

40. A smartly turned out D5604 cruises north with a return excursion from Brighton to Hitchin, on 29th May 1960. The main entrance to the station is visible below the left buffer of the locomotive. (S.C. Nash)

41. An overnight special, the 18.15 Newcastle to Hove, waits for the 10.25 Victoria to Littlehampton service on 4th June 1965. The locomotive is 2–8–0 no. 48544. The goods yard on the right had eight sidings and was closed on 11th November 1970. (J. Scrace)

42. This signal box replaced its two predecessors in 1932 and was surprisingly of traditional pitched roof style at a time when the SR was apparently obsessed by flat roofs. It too became redundant in 1983.
(E. Wilmshurst)

43. Icicles in railway tunnels are not unusual but in January 1985 a freezing wind from the north blew continuously for several weeks, straight through Haywards Heath tunnel. Services had to be suspended for a time while engineers attempted to ensure safety by removing many tons of ice from the ventilation shaft. (British Rail)

44. Nearly 1½ miles south of Haywards Heath, Folly Hill Box stood on the down side. It was built in 1908 to replace one of the tall "boxes on stilts" and survived until colour light signals arrived in 1932. (Late E. Wallis)

45. The brick base of the box survived to be adapted as a PW hut. Class H2 no. 32421 *South Foreland* speeds past it, with the rear coaches of a Birmingham to Brighton relief train passing under Rocky Lane bridge, on 23rd July 1955. (S.C. Nash)

WIVELSFIELD

46. The first station in the area was on the Lewes branch. This one was opened on the main line on 1st August 1886 and was known as Keymer Junction until 1st July 1896. Following heavy rain in October 1886, about 40ft of the new up platform collapsed down the embankment, taking the waiting room with it. (Lens of Sutton)

47. Thick fog blanketed the Weald as the 5.35pm up Newhaven boat train pulled away from a signal stop on 23rd December 1899. The crew of the up semi-fast train from Brighton failed to observe the very tall signals through the fog and their class B2 4–4–0, no. 206 *Smeaton*, ran into the rear of the boat train at about 40mph, resulting in six fatalities. (Lens of Sutton)

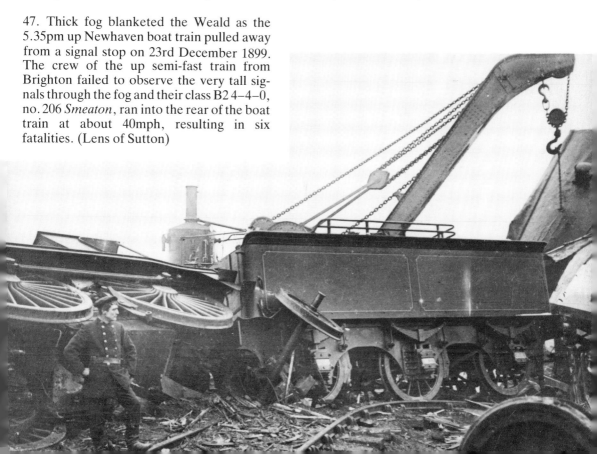

48. The signal box is seen at the north end of
the down platform, close to the bridge over
the road. Although the rails are at a great
height above the road, the head room in the
arch is only 13'9". (Lens of Sutton)

50. A southward view shows that the line
runs from embankment to cutting within the
length of the station. It also shows the SR
style nameboards and junction signals.
(Lens of Sutton)

49. Further problems with the stability of the
embankment have arisen. This photograph
was taken at the north end of the station on
3rd February 1913. (British Rail)

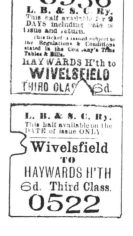

51. Class H2 no. 32424 *Beachy Head* passes through the cutting between the station and the junction on 13th April 1958 with a RCTS special to Newhaven. (E. Wilmshurst)

52. The passenger approach is most unusual. Two sets of covered steps lead up from the road and are connected together by a subway under the platforms. On the down side, passengers pass through the station building which contains the booking office. It is of similar design to those at Selham, Fittleworth and Hampden Park. (D. Cullum)

SOUTHERN RY.
Available on the DATE of issue ONLY
This Ticket is issued subject to the Regulations
& Conditions stated in the Company's Time
Tables & Bills.
WIVELSFIELD
TO
BURGESS HILL *b.h.*
THIRD CLASS.
1½d.   Fare   1½d.

53. A look north from the road bridge in 1983, shows that the line is now signalled for reversible running, there being two junction signals on the gantry. Trailing and facing crossovers add operating flexibility. The train is the 16.30 Redhill to Brighton service, headed by no. 73120. (J.S. Petley)

54. The LBSCR delighted to have its signal boxes on stilts. The exceptional height of this one enabled the signalman to see over the road bridge. It remained in use until about 1912. The little white post sticking out of the bank on the right carries, on this side, the name of Ganger Beard, whose responsibility for the permanent way begins at this point. (British Rail)

55. The replacement box was squat so that its staff could see *under* the bridge. This photograph of it was taken in 1932. A proposal had been made in 1881 to spend £35,000 on a flyover junction but it never came about. (Late E. Wallis)

56. The original Keymer Junction station was situated on the curve between the footbridge and the locomotive of this up train from Brighton. A further signal box can be seen beyond the footbridge. This controlled the level crossing in Cants Lane and eventually the junction itself. In March 1959, it was fitted with a prototype signalling panel but it became redundant with the recent resignalling scheme. (Lens of Sutton)

BURGESS HILL

57. A drawing dated 1843 gives an impression of the station which was originally some distance to the south of the road bridge. A hut similar to the one on the left survives today. In front of it, a railway policeman appears to be stopping a down train. As an economy measure, the station was closed from October 1843 to May 1844. In 1848, a waiting room was added, on the down side, at a cost of £15. (NRM)

The 1910 map shows the original sidings on the east side and those from 1889 on the west. The entire yard was closed in 1964.

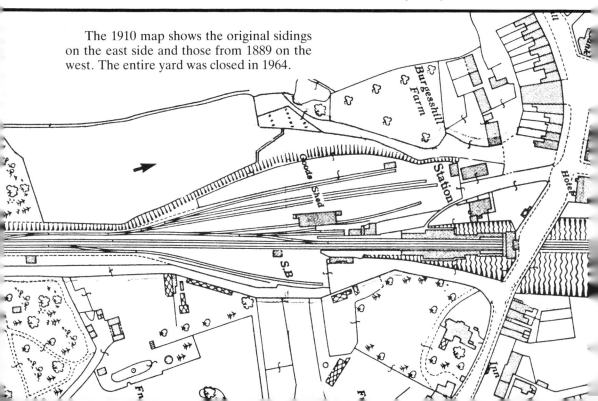

58. A new station was built at road level in 1877 but the earlier buildings were retained. This photograph of it is thought to date from 1910. In 1986 plans were submitted for redevelopment, which included erection of a DIY superstore. (Lens of Sutton)

59. Details of this impressive conflagration have not survived but it is believed to be an oil store blaze in 1906. The obverse reads simply "I think almost all Burgess Hill was there, as it was a great treat." The punctured hoses are lying across the main running lines. (R.C. Riley collection)

60. Class B4 no. 60 *Kimberley* heads the heavy 8.10am from Brighton. This train was unofficially known as "The Breadwinner". The graceful signal box was situated astride the goods shed road, 100 yards from the end of the up platform. (Bluebell Archives)

61. A photograph taken from the up starting signal in 1930 shows a deviation in the up siding where the signal box earlier straddled the track. In the foreground – period taxis. In the background – the South Downs. Pleasure gardens were opened nearby in 1898 and this attracted many passengers from Brighton. (Late E. Wallis)

0421

L. B. & S. C. Ry.

Red Hill Jun.

TO

BURGESS HILL

Third Cl. 3s. 3d

62. The history of many stations can be read from their platform edges. The brickwork on the left belongs to the 1877 alterations, whilst the stone blocks beyond belong to a much earlier period. They carry marks of having borne iron chairs 10½ x 5ins. and were probably used to carry the main line before the introduction of timber sleepers. (Lens of Sutton)

63. In 1986, the platform canopies remained standing, although devoid of their ornate valances. The historic shed on the left no longer served as a parcel store but one hopes it will survive as a memorial to the part the railway has played in the development of the town. (D. Cullum)

65. The SR seemed to have an obsession with lavatories when it came to selecting code letters for their electric stock. This is one of the 4LAV sets used on stopping services for over 30 years and is seen on 19th September 1966 in the company of "Late turn Patrick", a character well known to many local railway travellers. (J.H. Aston)

← 64. The covered footbridge is reputed to have been moved from Clapham Junction during alterations there in 1910. On the right are the previous down side buildings which served as offices for the coal merchant for many years. They have unfortunately recently been demolished along with the station master's house on the opposite platform. (Lens of Sutton)

HASSOCKS

66. There was no village of Hassocks before the railway arrived – just an area of heathland known as The Hassocks. This substantial station was provided on the up side, to the design of David Mocatta and the town eventually developed. (Lens of Sutton)

Hassocks : Hudson's Sand Siding.—This Siding is connected by hand points with the North end of the Sand Road in Goods Yard at which end there is a clearance sufficient for engine and eight trucks only. The Siding extends about ¾ mile from the Goods Yard connection and is shunted by the Ordinary Goods Service. Unless the exigencies of traffic working render it unavoidable, tender engines must not be used on the Siding, which is on a sharply falling gradient from the Goods Yard.

When entering the Siding a red flag must be fixed on the gate and remain there while the engine is in the Siding. When returning from the Siding, the Engine whistle must be sounded before reaching the rising gradient to the Goods Yard and one of the Good Staff must then see everything is clear and warn men engaged on the wharves, after which he must replace the red flag on the gate by a green flag and until this is seen, the engine must not start up the gradient for the Goods Yard. There is a gate at the Company's boundary and this must be closed after shunting is completed.

The 1910 edition shows the line to Stonepound Sand Pit. It passed close to the present tennis courts and under the A273 in a brick arch. Another point of interest is the cattle market on the down side. Sales were held weekly for many years. The extensive sidings were used for marshalling freight trains to and from different parts of the Sussex coast.

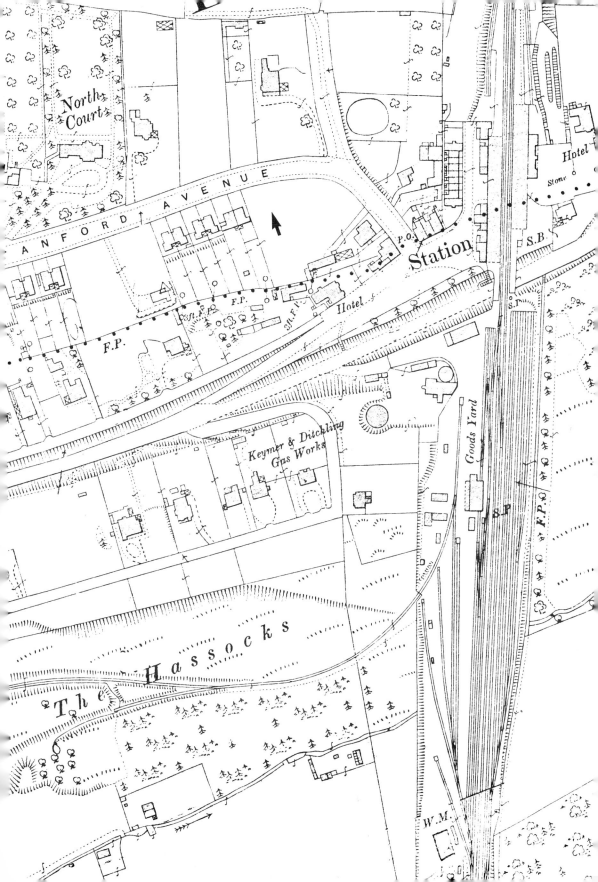

North Court

ANFORD AVENUE

Hotel
Stone

P.O.

S.B.

Station

S.P.

Hotel

F.P.

F.P.

F.P.

F.P.

Goods Yard

Keymer & Ditchling
Gas Works

S.P.

F.P.

S.P.

The Hassocks

W.M.

68. Relief signalman E. Walton poses in his box on 21st June 1930. The box remained in use after electrification but was then only manned part time, when access to the sidings was required. (Late E. Wallis)

67. Originally called Hassocks Gate after the tollgate at Stonepound, the "Gate" was dropped when the station was rebuilt and officially opened on 15th August 1881. This is the down side after creepers had obscured some of the ornamental plasterwork. The rebuilding was undertaken by Longleys who were not told that the platforms were on a gradient – the canopies finished one foot too low at one end! (Lens of Sutton)

69. Another photograph taken on the same day shows the extensive stock sidings and, on the extreme left, part of the gas works erected by LBSCR in 1863, which generated coal gas to illuminate the station and the signals as far south as Patcham Tunnel. The gas works formerly stood at Kingston Wharf, near Shoreham. (Late E. Wallis)

70. The up side buildings show that they were built to the same basic plans as those on the Cuckoo Line, the present Bluebell Line and the Midhurst to Lavant section. This shows their condition in September 1961. (D. Cullum)

71. The spacious platforms were sheltered by graceful canopies, which resounded impressively to passing expresses. This is the down side, looking north in January 1972. Only W.H. Smith's bookstall survived the destruction; it now enjoys a new life on Horsted Keynes platform on the Bluebell Railway. (E. Wilmshurst)

L. B. & S. C. RY.
This half available for 2 Days including Date of issue and return.
See conditions at Back

HAYWARDS HEATH. TO HASSOCKS
First Cl. 1s. 5d.

72. Here we see that the station remained intact in 1972 and that its predecessor was still standing. The latter survived as a cottage until the following year. The platforms now bear featureless glass structures, their only merit being minimum maintenance costs. The horizontal board at the end of the up platform was erected after drivers had mistaken a green down signal in the distance for the guard's hand lamp. (J. Scrace)

74. The reason for the castellated northern portal of Clayton tunnel remains uncertain. One theory was that as a castle was a symbol of strength and security – it gave confidence to the early traveller, fearful of a tunnel over 1¼ miles long. Another was more practical – an invading force from Europe was expected to first take the Weald and then advance north and south. Terrier no. 55 is seen taking the first rolling stock to the Bluebell Railway, on 17th May 1960. (S.C. Nash)

73. Remembrance class 4–6–4T no. 332 was built at Brighton in March 1922 and repainted in SR Maunsell green in November 1925. It is therefore seen between those dates, running south from Hasscoks with one of the all Pullman trains for which the line was famous for so many years.
(Lens of Sutton)

75. The southern portal was relatively plain but cluttered by a tiny signal cabin, surmounted by an ugly stove pipe. The summit of the line is nearby and was the scene of the frightful accident on 25th August 1861 when, owing to the primitive signalling, a rear end collision took place in the tunnel. The horrific and gory details have been recounted many times before. (D. Cullum collection)

76. This is Brapool Cutting box which was situated 900 yards north of Patcham Tunnel. A similar block post was provided at Clayton Cutting box, which was 600 yards south of that tunnel. No. 71, a class B4, is seen with the down "Pullman Limited" in about 1910. (Lens of Sutton)

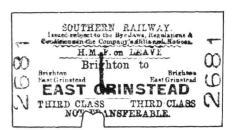

78. A visitor to the north end of the 492yd long Patcham Tunnel in March 1955 could have witnessed the passage of the Hastings to Birkenhead train. It had reversed at Brighton and is seen here behind ex-SECR class D no. 31737. The coaches were built in 1936 and the locomotive in 1901. The latter is now in York Railway Museum. (P. Hay)

77. The "Brighton Festival Belle" ran on 28th April 1982 and was hauled by no. 73101 *Brighton Evening Argus*. The Pullman coaches are those used on the UK leg of the revived Venice Simplon Orient Express and are seen running on the down line, between the tunnels. (J.S. Petley)

79. Another view of the north end shows the 14.14 London Bridge to Brighton service on 27th April 1967. Fine views of the South Downs are to be had in this part of the journey. (J. Scrace)

80. This small box was located on the down side 400yds south of the Tunnel. It is seen in 1932, not long before the end of its life. (Late E. Wallis)

PRESTON PARK

81. The LBSCR originated the "slipping" of coaches in 1858 and practised it almost as frequently as the GWR. Two guards were provided on the train – one disconnected the rear portion at speed and brought it to a standstill at the next station. Here the Worthing part of a down train has been released, whilst the main train runs non-stop through Preston Park. The raw chalk indicates where the cutting is being widened to provide more siding space.
(M.G. Joly collection)

82. The station was opened on 1st November 1869 to serve an expanding residential area. No doubt there was considerable local traffic to Brighton. This 1898 view shows the North Box on the left. (Lens of Sutton)

Preston Park : Down Local and Loop Lines.—Down Passenger Trains not calling at Preston Park must not be turned into the Loop Line or on to the Down Local Line, but any Train which has stopped at this Station may be sent down the Main or Local Line according to circumstances. As far as possible, all Down Goods Trains for Brighton must be turned to the Loop Line or Local Line, after being brought nearly to a stand.

83. The exhaust emerges sharply as class H1 no. 40 lifts its heavy train up the 1 in 264 gradient on the first part of the journey to London Bridge. (E.R. Lacey collection)

84. Looking north from the South Box up home signals, we have the opportunity to see the operating flexibility given to the signalman in that box. The two tracks in the left foreground are for direct Worthing trains running via the Cliftonville spur and the one on the right is the "down local" which commenced at Preston Park North – see next picture. (Late E. Wallis)

85. "King Arthur" class no. 795 *Sir Dinadan* blasts past the North Box, not long before the class was displaced from the route. Conductor rail insulating posts appear to be stacked in front of the signalman's privy.
(Lens of Sutton)

0403
L. B. & S. C. RY.
CHEAP TICKET.
Available only on day of
sue by trains as per Bill, and
the Stations named hereon,
ut not at Stations short of,
r beyond them.
VICTORIA TO
PRESTON PARK
FIRST CL 10s.0d.
See conditions at back.

86. The last N class to be built, no. 31414, drifts down the gradient on a sunny Sunday in April 1952 with an excursion from the London Midland Region. Electric stock is berthed in the up sidings, as it is Sunday. On the right is the station house – the offices were at a lower level. (P. Hay)

87. After an absence of several years, Brighton now has a regular daily service to Manchester. It is pictured here on 5th April 1983, behind no. 47486 which would take it to Willesden Junction, for electric haulage northwards. (J. Scrace)

89. The tunnel is almost straight, the curves being at either end. K class 2-6-0 no. 32338 is seen at the south end, in March 1954. (P. Hay)

88. The Cliftonville Spur, on the right, was opened on 1st July 1879 and has a 535yd long tunnel for nearly half its length. The mid-Victorian business travellers of Worthing were so frustrated by the enforced reversals at Brighton that they sought an Act of Parliament to construct the short line themselves. The LBSCR was thus "spurred" into action. The carriage sheds at the divergence of the lines became the Pullman Car Works in 1929. (Late E. Wallis)

90. Lovers Walk signal box was opposite the Stanford Road school, just north of the LBSCR paint shops, now the electric maintenance depot. This 1882 photograph shows the replacement box being erected and no. 392, a 2–4–0T of 1858 which was scrapped in 1889. (E.R. Lacey collection)

91. A well known view from above Lovers Walk box is worth repeating in large form. Locomotives line up in the afternoon sun prior to hauling return Bank Holiday excursions in 1871 or 72. Other points of interest are the disc signal, the wagons standing on the incline to the lower goods yard and the lack of buildings around the London Road viaduct. (Lens of Sutton)

92. A view up the steep gradient of New England Road. (R.C. Riley collection)

93. A view from Terminus Road in 1871 shows Montpelier Junction box at the divergence of the Lewes lines and a dainty narrow platform alongside locomotive and carriage works at which down trains stopped for ticket collection. This was done outside many termini at the time and was a source of great annoyance to passengers, particularly as the benefits of corridors were not available. (Lens of Sutton)

94. Looking down New England Road in 1858, we see through the original arches to the cast iron bridge which was erected in 1852 to take the lines into the lower goods yard. On the right is the locomotive works and its approach road, which crossed the main lines on the level. On the skyline is Cutress' Tower Mill in Ditchling Road and a signal, rotated to face the Lewes line. (O.J. Morris/E.R. Lacey collections)

95. The development of signalling in the Brighton area is a complex story. Most of the boxes on stilts were built with the signal posts integral with them, as we see here at Brighton Yard box, opposite the locomotive works in about 1872.
(Late E. Wallis collection)

96. The interior of the box is spartan, with only a wooden bench for staff comfort. Many of the wires pass out through the roof. (Late E. Wallis collection)

L. B. & S. C. Ry.
Available on the DATE of issue ONLY.
SEE CONDITIONS AT BACK.
BRIGHTON
TO
HAYWARD'S HEATH*h.h*
1s. 0d. THIRD CL. 1s. 0d.
8718

L. B. & S. C. RY.
Available on the DATE of issue ONLY.
This Ticket is issued subject to the Regulations
& Conditions stated in the Company's Time
Tables & Bills.
BRIGHTON
No. 2] TO
PORTSLADE po
3d. THIRD CLASS. 3d.
0462 10462

L. B. & S. C. RY,
Available on the DATE of issue ONLY.
This Ticket is issued subject to the Regulations
& Conditions stated in the Company's Time
tables & Bills.
BRIGHTON
Series 82] TO [Series 82
VICTORIA v.
THIRD CLASS.
6s. 3½d. Actual Fare. 6s. 3½d.
9791

L. B. & S. C. & L. & S. W. RYS.
Available for 2 days including date of issue
BRIGHTON to EASTLEIGH
Via HAVANT & L. & S. W. Ry.
4s. 9½d. THIRD CLASS. 4s. 9½d.
The connection of trains not guaranteed
Not Transferable. Issued subject to the
Conditions in the Time Tables of the respective
Cos over whose lines this ticket is available
EASTLEIGH
SINGLE
9031

97. Lying snow helps to emphasise the position of the turntables at the ends of the passenger platforms. These were used for removing vans, horseboxes or private carriage trucks from passenger trains, for unloading elsewhere. (Lens of Sutton)

paint dry. Goods stock and horse-drawn road vehicles are cordonned off by a line of carriages, while locomotives dry on the far left. (G.F. Collins collection)

99. From left to right – class E3 no. 166 *Cliftonville*, class B2 no. 314 *Charles C. Macrae*, class D3 no. 390 *St. Leonards* and a Shand Mason fire engine stand outside the works. There is still plenty to see for those who prefer signals to locomotives. (E.R. Lacey collection)

100. A view north from the South Box in July 1924 gives an opportunity to study contemporary rolling stock and signal detail. The paint shop is on the left, Montpelier Junction box is in the centre and the locomotive works are on the right. (Late E. Wallis)

101. Looking from the east it is clear how the locomotive works was extended on piers partly over the line to the lower goods yard. The area is now largely occupied by the biggest car park in the Southern Region. (Lens of Sutton)

102. An EMU from Victoria via Redhill approaches the terminus on 17th June 1961 at the same time as BR class 4 2–6–4T no. 80067 arrives with three coaches from Tunbridge Wells. "Battle of Britain" class no. 34089 *Squadron* leaves on the up line. (R.S. Greenwood)

103. A 1975 photograph shows the Upper Goods box, which controlled traffic between Upper Yard and Lower Yard, and was not a block post. In April 1986, the timber part was moved bodily to the Bluebell Railway for re-use at Sheffield Park. Until 1852, access to the Lower Yard had been from the Hove line only, via a tunnel under the main lines. (J. Scrace)

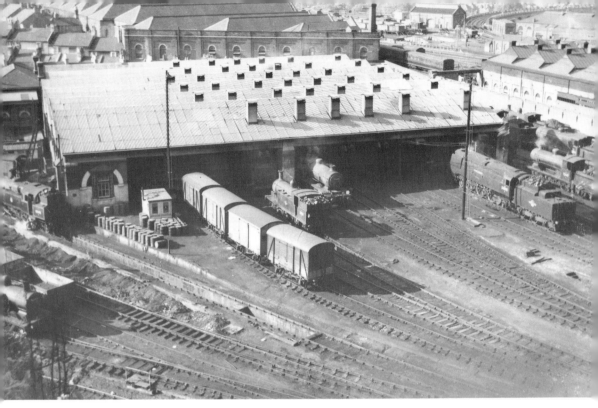

104. The motive power depot was situated between the main lines and the West Coast lines, in an area now occupied by the Combined Engineering Depot. Originally the roof was pitched in the opposite direction and access was through ten arches, one of which is seen on the left. This is a 1960 view, when there were 10 diesel shunters and 66 steam locomotives allocated to the depot. (J. Scrace)

105. Turning eastwards, the roof of the other running shed is evident, behind the massive water tank and water treatment plant. The 1932 signal box can be seen on the right, set in over the boiler shop. The relay room was badly damaged by fire on 1st October 1984, necessitating hand signalling for a week and reduced services for a further two weeks. The photograph was taken in March 1948. (D. Clayton)

106. Another look over the wall of Terminus Road (in 1961), a little further south, gives an indication of the dimensions of the former locomotive works. In 1896 there was a staff of 2200 (including crews) and 12 locomotives were built annually. The last was turned out in March 1957, one of a batch of 130 class 4 2-6-4Ts, although there was a period between the wars when none was produced. (D. Cullum)

BRIGHTON STATION

107. Improvements in 1861-62 included lengthening of the platforms (eliminating the turntables seen earlier) and provision of the clock tower in the centre of this picture, which dates from about 1880. The present train sheds were erected over their predecessors – both can be seen together in picture no.1 in our *Brighton to Worthing* album. (Lens of Sutton)

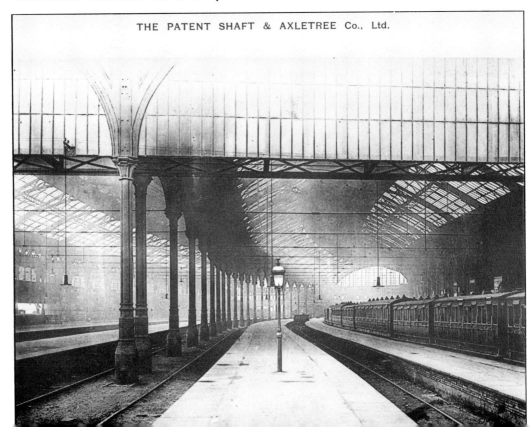

THE PATENT SHAFT & AXLETREE Co., Ltd.

109. W.H. Smith was operating a newspaper distribution business in London before the advent of railways. With their coming he and his son (also W.H.) arranged bookstall franchises with many of the large railway companies. Their association with Brighton is therefore of long standing. (Lens of Sutton)

← 108. The engineer for the reconstruction of the overall roof is often named but seldom is the contractor for the steelwork. This illustration is from one of their publications. Shafts and axletrees were important parts of horse-drawn carts. (P. Hay collection)

110. The company knew from bitter experience the problems of fire as their Brighton permanent way depot had been burnt down on 29th July 1861. This machine is steam-powered but horse-drawn. A cast iron notice proclaimed "No vehicle heavier than a horse cab allowed on this wooden decking". (P. Hay collection)

PLATFORMS
3.4 & 5
MAIN & EAST CO

fouling bar" – a flange-operated treadle, just
short of the buffers – which gave a platform
occupied indication to the signalman.
(Lens of Sutton)

112. An interesting view from platform 2 prior to electrification shows the complexity of the trackwork and signalling. On the left is one of the locomotive running sheds. Next is the West Box, which partly obscures the South Box – seldom were two boxes so close. (Lens of Sutton)

113. Electric services to London and West Worthing commenced on 1st January 1933 and on 14th March the SR held an exhibition in the station. No. B172 was the last of the B1 "Gladstone" class to be built. It was introduced in April 1891 and was the last to be withdrawn – six months after the show. (Lens of Sutton)

114. Mocatta's 1842 terminal building, with clock and balustrades (although devoid of its colonnade), still stands sandwiched between the 1882 train sheds and the porte cochère, of similar date. Also seen are the cream and black taxis, in their wartime guise with white painted bumpers and single headlights, in 1945. Other vintage transport items visible include the trolleybus, with its overhead equipment and the redundant terminal tram track. (NRM)

115. Two 4LAV sets leave for Victoria via Redhill on 29th June 1946. The photograph was taken from the unusual staff footbridge seen in photograph no.105. It had been created in 1932 from the obsolete signal gantry shown in picture no.100. (H.C. Casserley)

116. Three 5-coach all Pullman sets were provided for the "Brighton Belle". They operated a non-stop service to Victoria, usually three return trips daily apart from the war years, until 30th April 1972. Many of the cars were preserved – it is now possible to travel in one on the Swanage Steam Railway for example. (J. Scrace)

117. On the extreme right are platforms 1 and 2, used exclusively by Coastway West services (a name introduced in 1972). Platform 3 is the only one used by east-west services. A daily return journey between Newhaven and Portsmouth was provided in 1966 and again in 1986. What a commercial leap forward an hourly Hasting - Portsmouth service would be. On the left, platform 10 was absorbed into the car park and platform 9 was lost in 1985. The photograph date is 30th March 1974. (A.A.F. Bell)

118. The lower yard was closed in October 1980 but was reopened temporarily for mail traffic during the final phase of the alterations to the track layout at the approach to the station. From 31st March to 28th April 1985, all trains to and from London were scheduled for reversal at Hove and during weekends and evenings, Coastway East services terminated at Falmer. No. 73126 is seen with the 17.49 to London Bridge. (S.C. Nash)

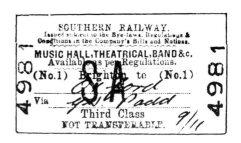

119. "Operation New Look" was the official title for the scheme. The New England Road bridge (by the cranes on the left) was completely rebuilt. All the turnouts were replaced by large radius high-speed points that no longer throw passengers from their feet upon arrival. The 1932 signal box (centre) presented a problem to the demolition contractors. A fire in the box in the previous year had badly disrupted services for many weeks. All operations are now controlled from Three Bridges. (J. Bloom)

120. The objective of millions of travellers on the Brighton line has been the seaside, with its beach and piers. The objective for railway historians must be the Volks Railway – the first public electric railway in Britain. It was opened on 4th August 1883, photographed here in 1949 and thankfully is still cared for by Brighton Corporation. (S.W. Baker)

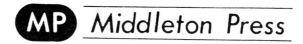

MP *Middleton Press*

Easebourne Lane, Midhurst, West Sussex, GU29 9AZ
☎ Midhurst (073 081) 3169

BRANCH LINES

BRANCH LINES TO MIDHURST	0 906520 01 0
BRANCH LINES TO HORSHAM	0 906520 02 9
BRANCH LINE TO SELSEY	0 906520 04 5
BRANCH LINES TO EAST GRINSTEAD	0 906520 07 X
BRANCH LINES TO ALTON	0 906520 11 8
BRANCH LINE TO HAYLING	0 906520 12 6
BRANCH LINE TO SOUTHWOLD	0 906520 15 0
BRANCH LINE TO TENTERDEN	0 906520 21 5
BRANCH LINES TO NEWPORT	0 906520 26 6
BRANCH LINES TO TUNBRIDGE WELLS	0 906520 32 0
BRANCH LINE TO SWANAGE	0 906520 33 9
BRANCH LINES AROUND GOSPORT	0 906520 36 3

SOUTH COAST RAILWAYS

BRIGHTON TO WORTHING	0 906520 03 7
WORTHING TO CHICHESTER	0 906520 06 1
CHICHESTER TO PORTSMOUTH	0 906520 14 2
BRIGHTON TO EASTBOURNE	0 906520 16 9
RYDE TO VENTNOR	0 906520 19 3
EASTBOURNE TO HASTINGS	0 906520 27 4
PORTSMOUTH TO SOUTHAMPTON	0 906520 31 2

SOUTHERN MAIN LINES

WOKING TO PORTSMOUTH	0 906520 25 8
HAYWARDS HEATH TO SEAFORD	0 906520 28 2
EPSOM TO HORSHAM	0 906520 30 4
CRAWLEY TO LITTLEHAMPTON	0 906520 34 7
THREE BRIDGES TO BRIGHTON	0 906520 35 3

STEAMING THROUGH

STEAMING THROUGH KENT	0 906520 13 4
STEAMING THROUGH EAST HANTS	0 906520 18 5
STEAMING THROUGH EAST SUSSEX	0 906520 22 3

OTHER RAILWAY BOOKS

WAR ON THE LINE The official history of the SR in World War II	0 906520 10 X
GARRAWAY FATHER AND SON The story of two careers in steam	0 906520 20 7

OTHER BOOKS

MIDHURST TOWN – THEN & NOW	0 906520 05 3
EAST GRINSTEAD – THEN & NOW	0 906520 17 7
THE MILITARY DEFENCE OF WEST SUSSEX	0 906520 23 1
WEST SUSSEX WATERWAYS	0 906520 24 X
BATTLE OVER PORTSMOUTH A City at war in 1940	0 906520 29 0